# NATURAL SCIENCE
# PRIMARY 2

BY ME

ACTIVITY BOOK


| | | |
|---|---|---|
| Unit 1 | How my body works | 2 |
| Unit 2 | Look after yourself | 8 |
| Unit 3 | The animal kingdom | 14 |
| Unit 4 | The plant kingdom | 20 |
| Unit 5 | Matter and forces | 26 |
| Unit 6 | Machines and energy | 32 |
| | Glossary | 38 |


CB123072

# UNIT 1 How my body works

**1 Match. Write *smell, hear, taste, see, touch.***

I see
with my eyes.

I ______
with my nose.

I ______
with my tongue.

I ______
with my ears.

I ______
with my fingers.

**2 Which sense are they using? Circle.**

She can **smell** / **taste** perfume.

He can **hear** / **touch** a cactus.

They can **see** / **hear** a rainbow.

We can **taste** / **hear** a trumpet.

## 3 Circle the body parts. Label the pictures.

smallintestinebrainteethheartlungsstomachlargeintestine

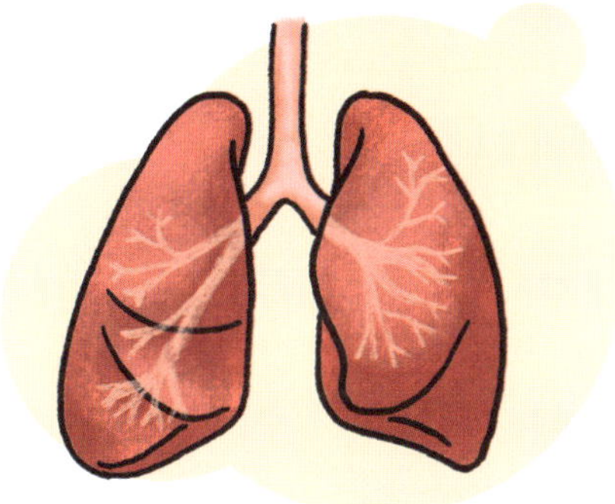

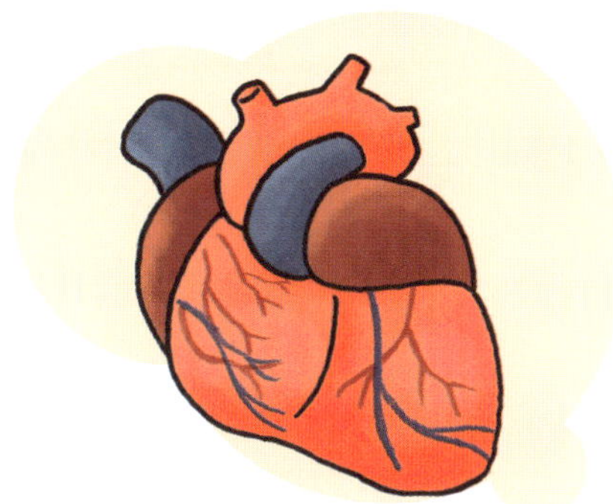

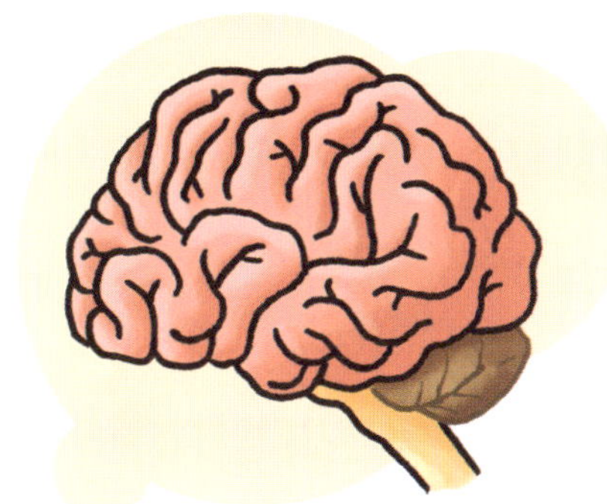

## 4 Label the digestive system. Use words from activity 4.

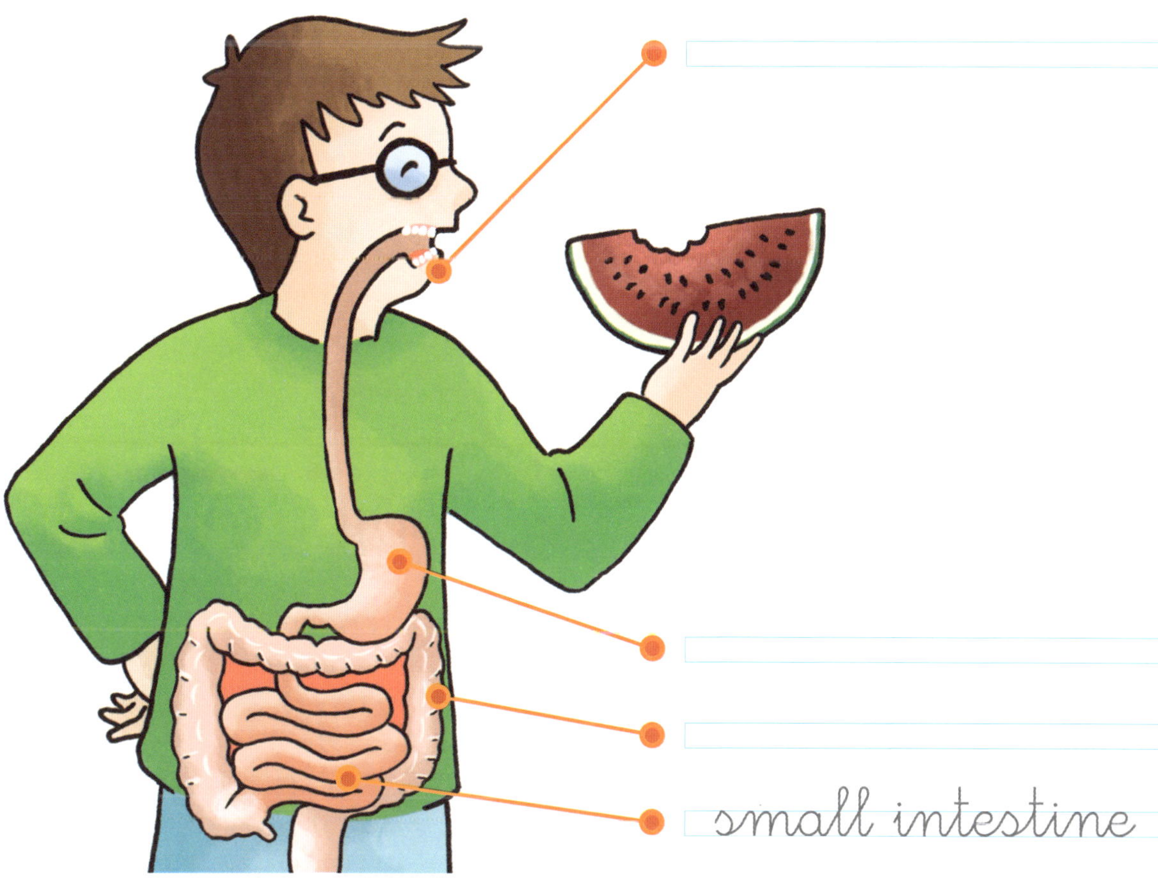

## 5 Match the sentences and pictures. Circle the joints.

1 He's kicking a ball.

2 He's scratching his head.

3 He's throwing a ball.

4 She's touching her toes.

A

knee wrist
elbow neck
shoulder

B

knee neck
wrist finger
toe

C

neck ankle
toe waist
shoulder

D

ankle elbow
shoulder
knee

## 6 Read. Write *true* or *false*.

A **joint** is where 2 **bones** join. True

The **skull** protects the **brain**. ______

Only arms have **muscles**. ______

**Muscles** work in pairs. ______

**Bones** grow. ______

## 7 Number in order of age. Write the words on the timeline.

adult

child

1

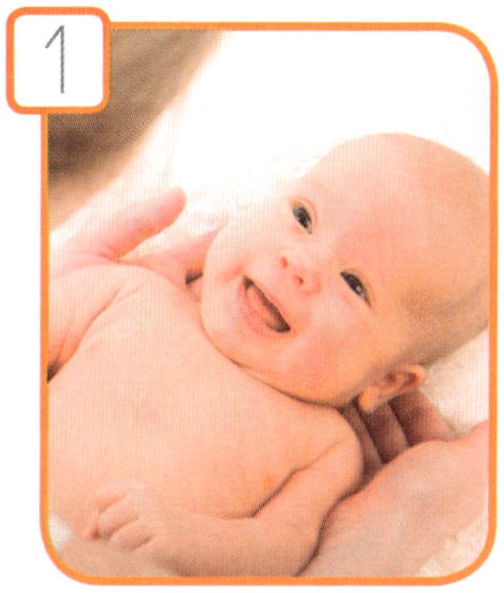

baby

adolescent

1 baby

2 ______

3 ______

4 ______

older adult

## 8 Match.

- I go to school.
- I get dressed on my own.
- I need a lot of help.
- I can't talk.
- I am studying Science in English!

# Let's investigate at home!

## Make a skeleton

1

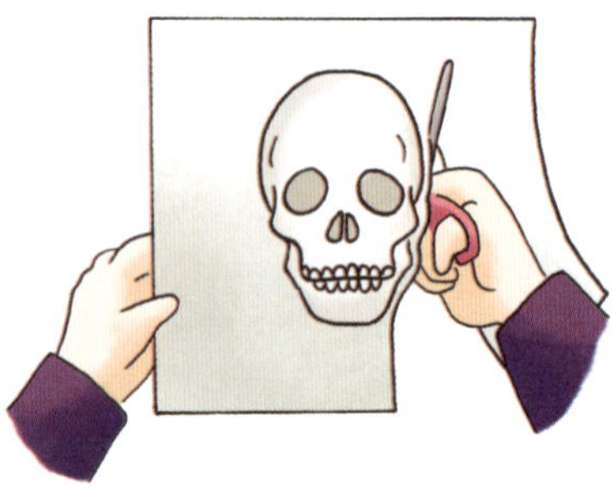

Draw a skull and stick on the black card.

2

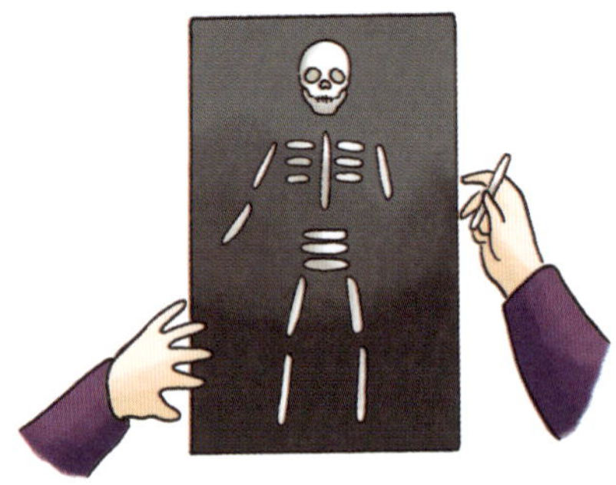

Use the earbuds to make the skeleton body.

3

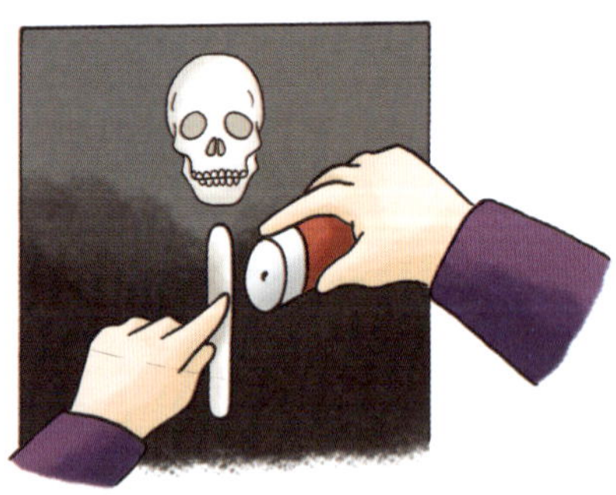

Glue the earbuds onto the card.

4

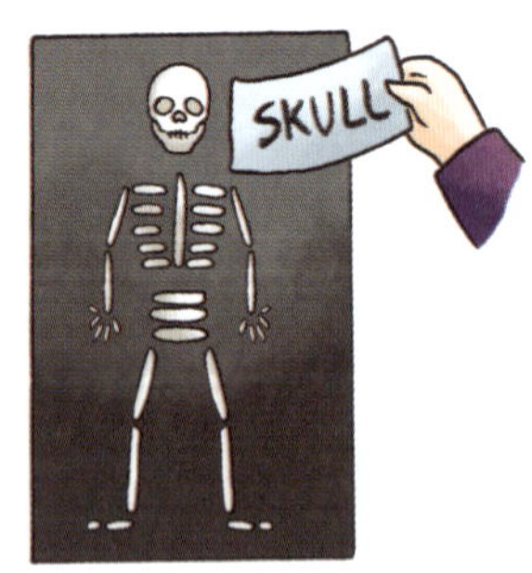


Label some of the bones and joints.

## 1 Find out.

How many bones do you have in your body? ____________

How many ribs do you have? ____________

## Skills check

**1** **Read the instructions. Draw and colour.**

Colour the small triangle orange.

Draw salty food in the big triangle.

Draw your favourite smell in the square.

Circle a loud noise.

Draw a soft object on the hand.

Draw what you can see outside the window.

Colour the chameleon your favourite colour.

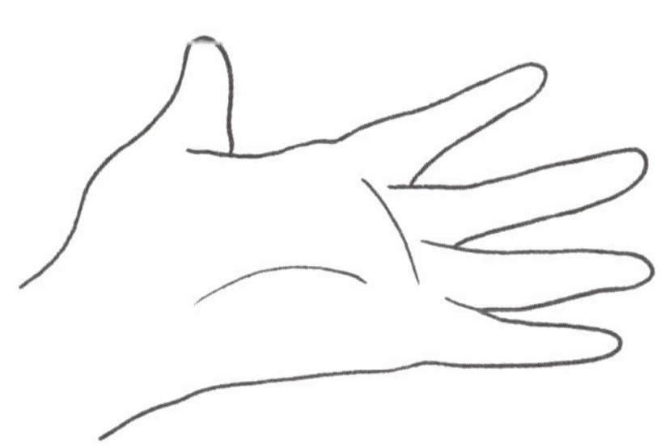

# UNIT 2 Look after yourself

1 Match the sentences with the boys or girls. Write the number.

1 Don't climb high trees!
2 Look and listen near roads.
3 Be careful with dogs!
4 Wear a helmet!
5 Don't fight!

2 Choose one piece of advice. Design your own sign.

Wear protection. Warm up for sport. Be alert.
Eat healthy food. Don't do dangerous activities.

3 What part of the body do they protect? Write.

knees head hands ~~eyes~~

They protect your eyes.

They protect your ________.

They protect your ________.

It protects your ________.

4 Write the words and use the code.

fat carbohydrate protein dairy product

O________ B________ M________ Y________

**5** Write a food diary. Write and draw what you had for breakfast, lunch and dinner today.

| my breakfast | my lunch | my dinner |
| --- | --- | --- |
| | | |

**6** Write.

He is playing ______.

They are ______.

He ______.

## 7 Complete the sentences about you.

less than 9 hours at night | more than 9 hours at night | with water | with soap and water | once a day | twice a day | three times a day

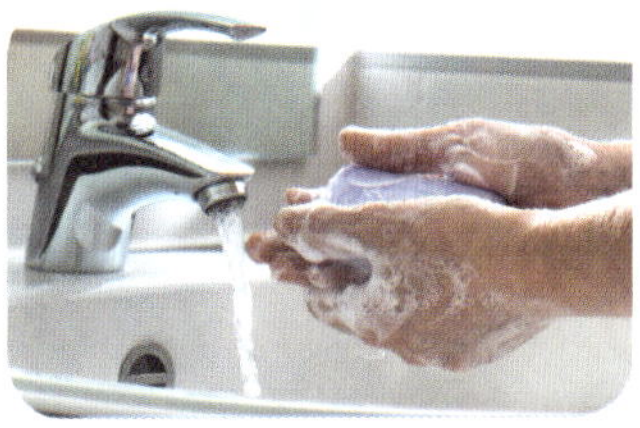

I wash my hands ______________________________

______________________________.

I sleep ______________________________

______________________________.

I brush my teeth ______________________________

______________________________.

## 8 Unjumble the sentences. Circle A or B.

blond hair got long he has — A (B)

He has got ...

glasses wearing he is — A B

______________________________

speak can he English — A B

______________________________

likes he football playing — A B

______________________________

A

B

# Let's investigate at home!

## Make a timeline chart

1

Take photos of people in your family.

2

Cut out the different family members.

3

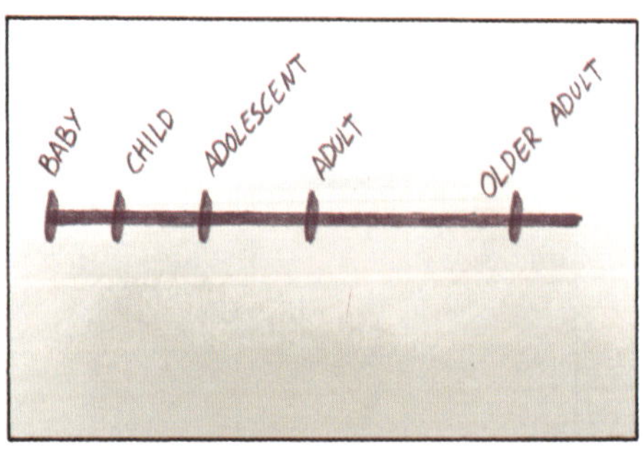


Draw a timeline and write the different stages.

4

Stick the photos in the correct place.

## 1 Write.

Who is the youngest person in your family? ______________________

Who is the oldest person in your family? ______________________

## Skills check

**1** Look at the picture. Read and write the name.

**Example:** She is eating sweet food. *Wendy*

1. He is touching a hot object. ____________
2. He has a bad stomach. ____________
3. She likes flying kites. ____________
4. She is eating something healthy. ____________
5. He is an adolescent. ____________

# UNIT 3 The animal kingdom

**1** **Which animal fits in the green box? Write the word and circle the picture.**

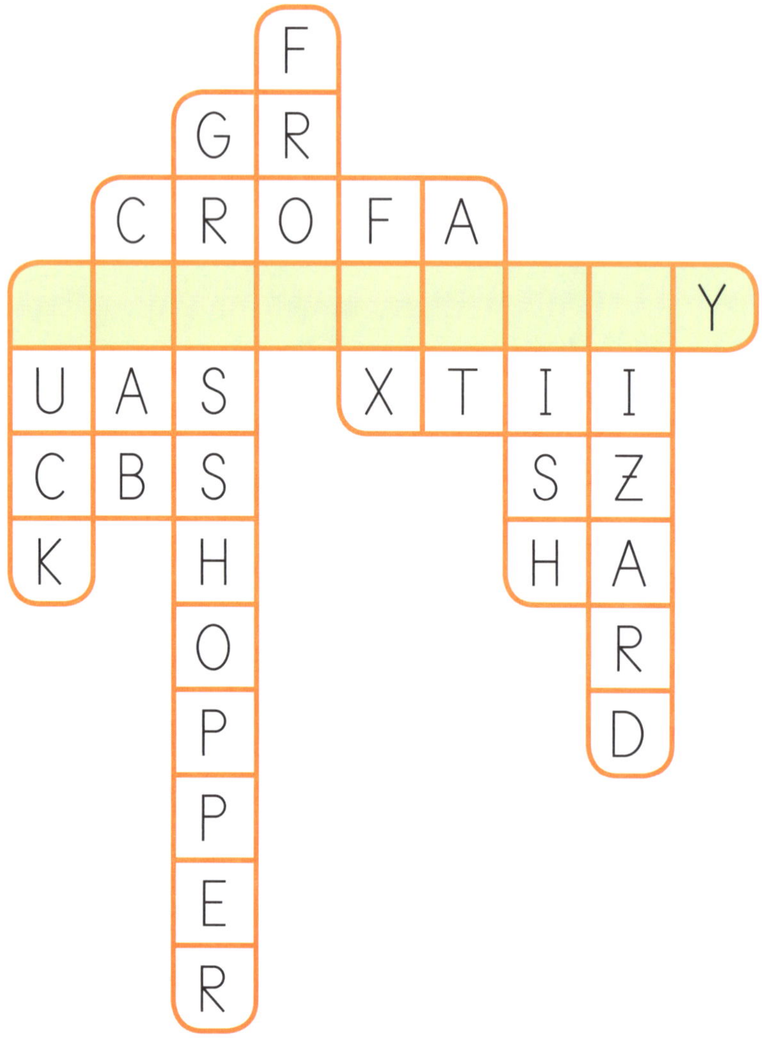

**2** **Choose two living things from the crossword in activity 1 to complete each sentence.**

a) A crab and ant can crawl.

b) A ______ and ______ can swim.

c) A ______ and ______ can run.

d) A ______ and ______ can jump.

e) A ______ and ______ can fly.

## 3 Read and write *invertebrates* or *vertebrates*.

They are ________________
because they have a backbone.

They are ________________
because they don't have a backbone.

## 4 Look at the vertebrates. Complete the words.

Mammals have f u r or h a i r.

Birds have f _ _ th _ rs and a b _ _ k.

Amphibians have m _ _ st sk _ n.

Reptiles have sc _ _ _ s.

Fish have g _ lls and f _ ns.

## 5 Read and put a tick or a cross.

| vertebrates | herbivore | carnivore | viviparous | oviparous |
|---|---|---|---|---|
|  panda | ✓ | | | |
|  crocodile | | | | |
|  trout | | | | |
|  zebra | | | | |
|  snake | | | | |
|  turtle | | | | |

## 6 Read about two arthropods. Write *butterfly* or *lobster*.

a It has 6 legs. butterfly

b It has 3 body segments. ______

c It has wings. ______

d It has a thick exoskeleton. ______

e It has claws. ______

**7** **Read and draw the molluscs in the correct place.**

Draw two **snails** on a leaf. Draw three **slugs** in the grass. Draw six **mussels** on the big rock and four **limpets** on the small rock. Draw two **squid** in the sea.

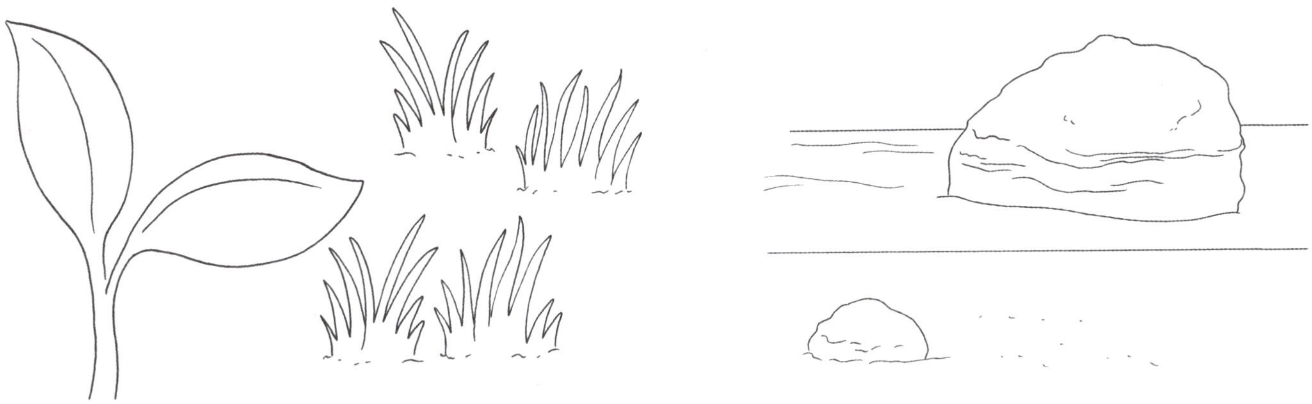

**8** **Complete the classification table with the animals in the box.**

lizard  snail  duck  spider  fox

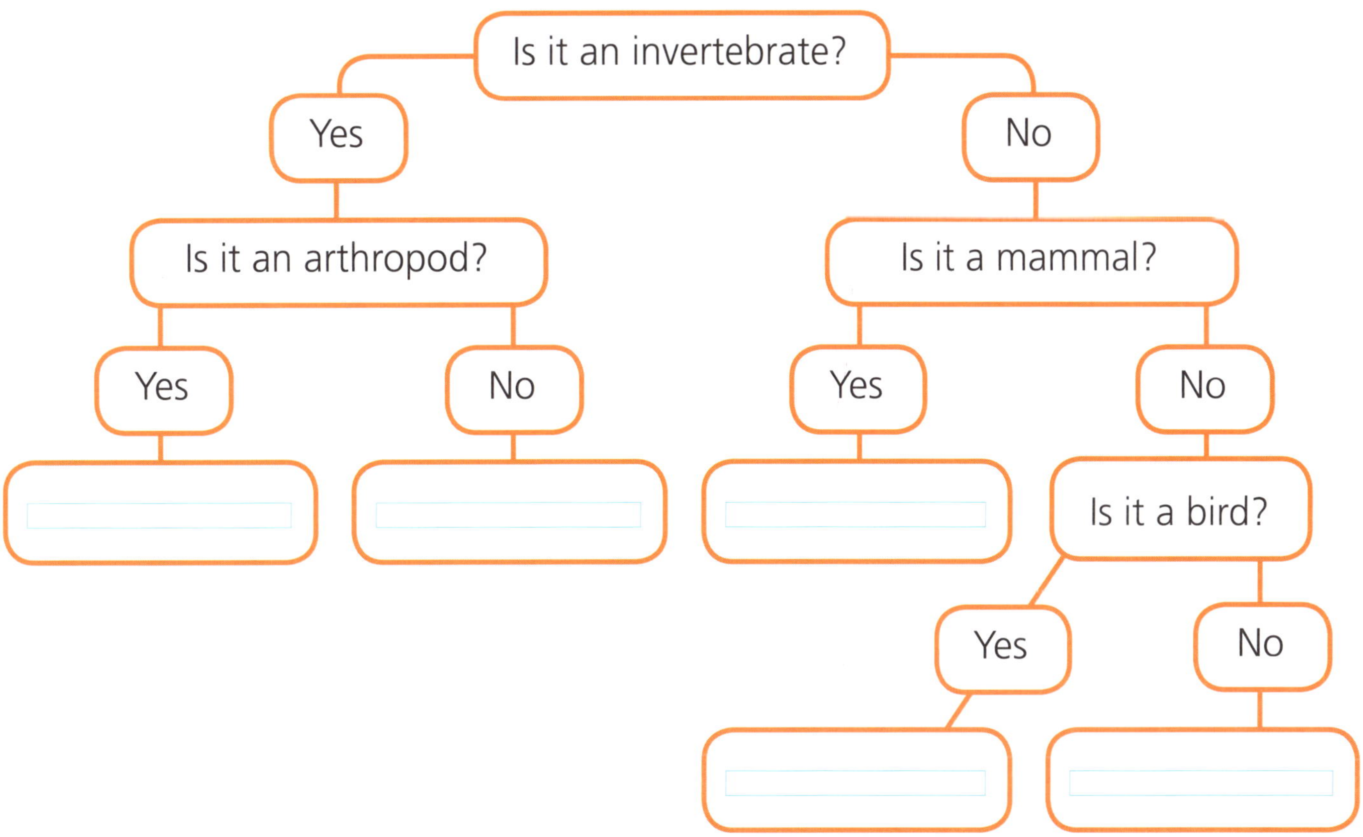

# Let's investigate at home!

## Make an animal diorama

1

Choose a group of animals.

2

Draw and cut out some of your animals.

3

Create a habitat inside a cardboard box.

4

Place or stick your animals inside your diorama.

1 Describe your diorama.

My animals are ____________________

They have ____________________

They eat ____________________

## Skills check

**1** **Look and read. Write the names of the animals. You can add more than one animal for each sentence.**

duck

salmon

crab

cow

elephant

frog

beetle

**Example:** It's viviparous — cow and elephant

1. It's a herbivore. __________
2. It has a hard exoskeleton. __________
3. It has scales. __________
4. It has feathers and wings. __________
5. It has a segmented body. __________
6. It has moist skin. __________

# UNIT 4 The plant kingdom

## 1 Write and match.

**Plants need…**

a ______ w ______ s ______

## 2 Colour.

● It needs water. ● It needs air.

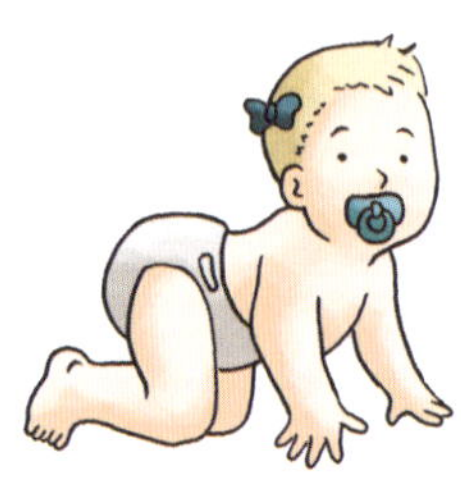

## 3 Look and write.

stem roots leaves seeds ~~flower~~

## 4 Look, write and circle.

| | grass | bush | tree |
|---|---|---|---|
|  apple tree | no<br>wild • cultivated | no<br>wild • cultivated | yes<br>wild • **(cultivated)** |
|  wheat | wild • cultivated | wild • cultivated | wild • cultivated |
|  blackberry | wild • cultivated | wild • cultivated | wild • cultivated |

5 **Draw and colour. Match.**

- Roots take up water.

- Leaves absorb sunlight.

- Flowers produce seeds.

## 6 Number in order of the process.

cotton fabric

1

cotton

T-shirt

chair

wood

pine tree

## 7 Draw the process for making orange juice.

1

2

3

## Let's investigate at home!

### What do seeds look like?

1

Draw the fruit on a sheet of card.

2

Draw and colour their leaves.

3

Cut the fruit in half and look at the seeds.

4

Draw and colour the seeds. Compare!

### 1 Write.

Are all the seeds the same size? ____________________

Are all the seeds the same shape? ____________________

Are all the seeds the same colour? ____________________

## Skills check

**1 Look and read. Put a tick or a cross. Look at the two examples.**

This is a bush. ✓

This is a grass. ✗

1 These are fruits. ☐

2 These are leaves. ☐

3 These are seeds. ☐

4 These are roots. ☐

5 This is a tree. ☐

# UNIT 5 Matter and forces

**1** Write the name of the object in the correct box.

doll

book

shirts

jar

hat

door

trumpet

notebook

pan

bottle

| It's made of wood. | It's made of glass. | It's made of fabric. |
|---|---|---|
| door | | |

| It's made of plastic. | It's made of metal. | It's made of paper. |
|---|---|---|
| | | |

**2** Write the properties of these objects.

| | | | |
|---|---|---|---|
| Is it soft or hard? |  soft |  |  |
| Is it transparent or opaque? | 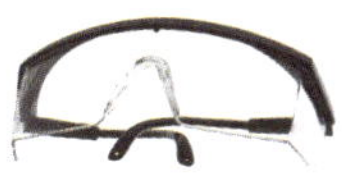 |  |  |
| Is it flexible or rigid? |  |  |  |
| Is it rough or smooth? |  |  |  |
| Is it absorbent or waterproof? |  |  |  |

**3** Draw an object. Write a description.

It's made of ______

It's ______

______

## 4 We change materials. Match. Write *R* for reversible changes.

We can...

- stretch it ☐
- bend it ☐
- squeeze it ☐ R
- heat it ☐
- freeze it ☐

## 5 Write the words in the correct column.

book

milk

apple

water

car

oil

| liquid | solid |
|---|---|
| milk | |
| | |
| | |

## 6 Do they mix well together? Write.

mix well together | don't mix well together

chocolate powder and milk

______________________.

rocks and water ______________

______________________.

## 7 Read and circle the correct options.

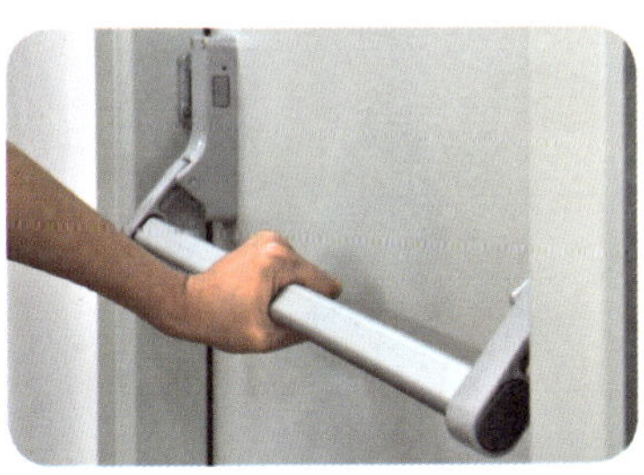

We pull things **away from us / towards us**. We can push and pull a door.

We push things **away from us / towards us**. We can push and pull a swing.

Some materials move towards a magnet. Magnets attract **metal objects / plastic objects**.

# Let's investigate at home!

## Make your own ice lollies

1

Wash your small yoghurt pots.

2

Pour your favourite juice into the pots with a little water.

3

Add the lolly sticks and put into the freezer.

4

Enjoy your frozen lollies with your friends.

## 1 True or false?

Freezing juice and water is reversible. ______

A lolly is a solid. ______

## Skills check

**1 Look and complete the description. Use a word from the box.**

transparent   rubber   irreversible   ~~glass~~   stretch   fabric   waterproof

It's made of glass.

1 

It's made of ______.

2 

It's made of ______.

3 

It is ______.

4 

It is ______.

5 

I can ______ it.

6 

This change is ______.

# Machines and energy

## 1 Circle the words in the *word snake* then label the tools.

spannerhammersawpliersscrewdriver

## 2 Look and circle the correct word.

1 

These tools help us **cut** / **join** / **lift** things.

2 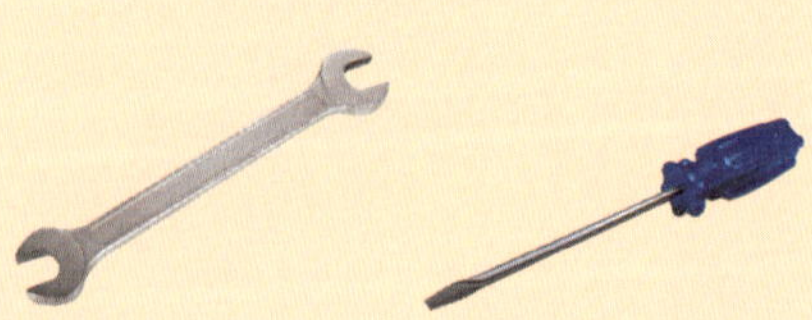

These tools help us **cut** / **join** / **lift** things.

3 

These tools help us **cut** / **join** / **lift** things.

## 3 Read and draw. Circle the complex machines.

There is a **toaster** and a **knife** in the kitchen. There is a **toothbrush** and a **mop** in the bathroom. There is a **hairdryer** in the bedroom and a **computer** in the living room.

| bathroom | bedroom |
| --- | --- |
| kitchen | living room |

## 4 Match the description with the tool or machine. Write the name.

We use it to...

a toast our bread.

b find information.

c wash the floors.

d clean our teeth.

e dry our hair.

mop

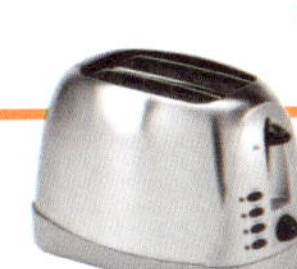

## 5 Write the name of the machine the people use.

walkie-talkie

tractor

trolley

hammer

I use a ______ to work on the farm.

Farmer

I use a ______ to fix your door.

Carpenter

I use a ______ to move boxes.

Delivery man

I use a ______ ______ to talk and communicate.

Police officer

## 6 Draw four machines you use every day and write their names.

1 ______

2 ______

3 ______

4 ______

## 7 Unjumble the letters. Label the picture.

b l e c a

__________

g l u p

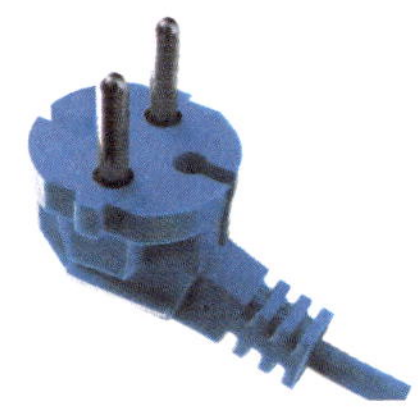

__________

t e k c o s

__________

t s a t e b i r e

__________

w i c s h t

__________

## 8 Write.

the Sun the wind water

Solar energy uses energy from __________.

Turbines use energy from __________.

Power stations use energy from __________.

# Let's investigate at home!

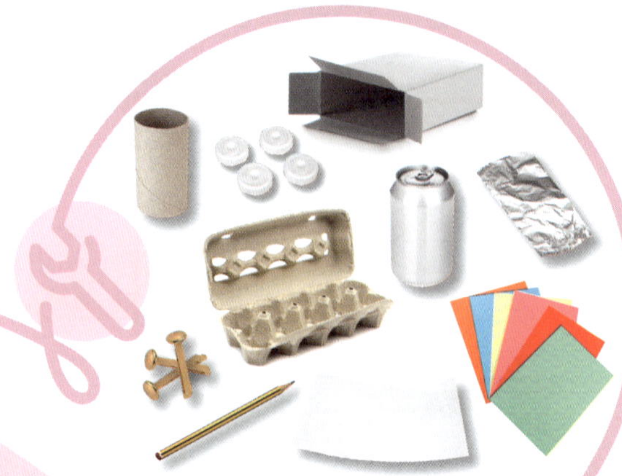

## Design and make a robot

1

Look at your materials. Design a robot.

2

Use aluminum foil and the box to make a body.

3

Add a head and a face.

4

Add arms and legs. How can you make them move?

## 1 Think about it.

Is your robot similar to a real boy or girl? ______________________

Is your robot similar to a real machine? ______________________

## Skills check

1 Look and read. Write *yes* or *no*.

**Example:** The oven is a complex machine. yes

1. The pot is hot. ______
2. A knife is a tool. ______
3. A phone is a simple machine. ______
4. A vacuum cleaner uses batteries. ______
5. An iron uses mains electricity. ______
6. The cable on the floor is dangerous. ______

# Glossary

| English | Your language |
| --- | --- |

## UNIT 1: How my body works

| | |
| --- | --- |
| senses | |
| teeth | |
| stomach | |
| small intestine | |
| large intestine | |
| heart | |
| lungs | |
| brain | |
| skeleton | |
| bone | |
| joint | |
| muscle | |

## UNIT 2: Look after yourself

| | |
| --- | --- |
| be alert | |
| be careful | |
| fats | |
| carbohydrates | |
| proteins | |
| dairy products | |
| fruit and vegetables | |
| healthy | |
| unhealthy | |
| meal | |
| exercise | |
| healthy habits | |

| English | Your language |
| --- | --- |

## UNIT 3: The animal kingdom

| | |
| --- | --- |
| skin | |
| fur | |
| feathers | |
| wings | |
| fins | |
| gills | |
| shell | |
| arthropod | |
| mollusc | |
| squid | |
| slug | |
| limpet | |

## UNIT 4: The plant kingdom

| | |
| --- | --- |
| sunlight | |
| air | |
| water | |
| tree | |
| bush | |
| grass | |
| root | |
| stem | |
| leaf | |
| flower | |
| seed | |
| fruit | |

# Glossary

| English | Your language |
|---|---|
| **UNIT 5: Matter and forces** | |
| wood | |
| sand | |
| cotton | |
| wool | |
| rubber | |
| opaque | |
| waterproof | |
| stretch | |
| bend | |
| squeeze | |
| freeze | |
| heat | |
| **UNIT 6: Machines and energy** | |
| spanner | |
| hammer | |
| pliers | |
| screwdriver | |
| join | |
| lift | |
| batteries | |
| mains | |
| cable | |
| plug | |
| switch | |
| socket | |